Mary and the Fireflies

By Mary Perrone Davis

Text and illustrations copyright © 2018 Mary Perrone Davis

All rights reserved. This book is protected under the copyright laws of the United States of America. This book may not be copied or reprinted for commercial gain or profit.

ISBN: 978-1-943523-51-1

Cover and Illustrations by: Grace Metzger Forrest (www.gracedesigns.me)

Published by Laurus Junior Series

Laurus Junior Series

Laurus Junior Series is an imprint of:
THE LAURUS COMPANY, INC.
www.TheLaurusCompany.com

Dedication

This book is dedicated to

all those who have shared

the light of Jesus with me,

even in their darkest moments.

There are too many of you to name,

but you know who you are,

and I love each of you.

Mary sat outside one evening.
As she swung her legs from her back porch,
she noticed small flashes of light
across her yard,
first here,
        then there.

Mary's curiosity got the best of her,
and she began to run
from one flash to another.

But as soon as
she neared a flash,
it seemed to disappear.

Frustrated, Mary called for her mother.

"What is it, Mary?" her mother asked
as she joined her in the yard.

"Look at all the flashing," Mary said
as she pointed around the yard.
"What's going on?"

"Oh, those are fireflies,"
explained Mary's mother.
"Let's try to catch one so we can
get a better look at it, but then
we will have to let it go."

Mary's mother went into the house
and returned with two jars.

Soon, Mary and her mother
were both running around the yard
swinging their jars.

Mary was the first to yell,
"I got one!"

"Quick, put the lid on,"
her mother said.

They sat down in the soft grass
with the jar between them.

"It sure is pretty when it's lit up,
but it doesn't look like anything
but an old bug when it's not,"
said Mary as she spread out on her belly
for a closer look.

"Remember how Jesus said to
let your light shine?"
Mary's mother asked her.

"God put His spark of light in each of us, but
we don't shine brightly all the time either."

"It's easy to see in some people, and
it's hidden in others. Most of us are
like fireflies who shine off and on."

"How do we shine?" asked Mary.

"We shine when we love,"
explained her mother.
"When we love others, we are a
reflection of God's love in us."

"I want to shine, too," Mary replied.

Mary took the lid off her jar.
As the firefly flew away,
Mary gave her mother a big hug.

Then she spread her arms, as if flying,
and ran around the yard singing,
"This little light of mine,
I'm gonna let it shine."

ABOUT THE AUTHOR

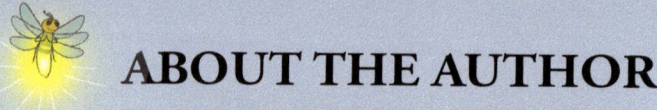

MARY PERRONE DAVIS is a wife, mother, grandmother, Lay Carmelite, Registered Nurse (working as a school nurse), and a children's author.

Mary never planned to be an author. She was spending some quiet time outside on a women's retreat when a butterfly landed nearby and her first book, ***Mary's Butterfly Garden***, was born.

She hopes that her love of The Lord is reflected in her books and in her life.

ABOUT THE ILLUSTRATOR

GRACE METZGER FORREST graduated from the Art Institute of Atlanta in 1990. Her career has included animating children's CDs—"making dinosaur eggs hatch and bean seeds grow." She has created animated mutating cells for the CDC, presentations for Coca-Cola Corp., video game scenes, and JELL-O creatures for Cartoon Network. One of her projects won a New Media Invision Bronze.

Grace works in her studio near the Chesapeake Bay and shares a "junior" farm with her husband and daughter, complete with a garden, brown eggs, and two goats.